VEDAS – IN A NUTSHELL

DR. JAGADEESH PILLAI

Made with ♥ on the Notion Press Platform
www.notionpress.com

This is a salute to those interested in exploring the basics of Vedas and Vedic knowledge.

Contents

Prayer

Ganga tharanga ramaneeya jata kalapam,
Gowri niranthara vibhooshitha vama bhagam,
Narayana priya mananga madapaharam,
Varanasi pura pathim Bhajha Viswanatham ||

About The Author

Dr. Jagadeesh Pillai four times Guinness World Record holder, a voracious reader, writer, and true research scholar was born in Varanasi, the abode of Lord Shiva. He is Ph.D. in Vedic Science. He is a multi-faceted polymath with innate qualities, creative ideas and many remarkable achievements. Although his roots extend back to "Gods own Country"(Kerala), the residents of Varanasi feel proud of him and adore him as a child of Varanasi who caters to every individual in need without any expectations. A deep study into his profile reflects that he has added so many feathers to his cap which makes him quite unique. He is a four times Guinness Book of World Records Holder in the following subjects :

1. "Script to Screen" which he achieved by producing and directing a state of art animation film within the shortest time possible by breaking the earlier set record by Canadians. There are many national and international Awards and Recognitions to his credit.

2. Longest Line of Post Cards which he has done on the occasion of 163 years of Indian Postal Day by 16300 post cards. The event was also connected with a questionnaire about Indian Flag.

3. Largest Poster Awareness Campaign – This was achieved by designing an awareness campaign on the subject "Beti Bachao – Beti Padhao".

4. Largest Envelop – Towards tribute to Prime Minister's

initiative 'Make in India' – he has created about 4000 sq meter envelop using waste papers.

5. Attempted by lighting 70000 candles on a 210 kg cake to celebrate the 70th Indian Independence day recorded in World Records India.

6. Attempted a documentary on Dhamek Stupa of Sarnath dubbing in 17 languages, result is waiting from Guinness World Records.

He is versatile in Gita teaching. The young generation is fond of his Gita teaching and he has changed the life of many young through his continued motivational boost up and teachings.

He has composed and sung Gayatri Mantra in 1000 different tunes.

He has composed and sung Hanuman Chalisa in 108 different tunes.

He has composed and sung hundreds of Sanskrit Bhajans, Patriotic songs, etc.

He has written and directed so many short films and documentaries for awareness campaigns.

He has done voluntary services to UP Police and Kerala Police to spread awareness campaigns on the various issue through videos and photography.

He is on the path of authoring thousands of books on Indian culture, Indian Temples, and the life of extraordinary people.

It is hard to believe that he has produced and directed more than 100 Documentaries on a particular city (Varanasi) which is done by a single person.

He has helped and guided more than 25 boys and girls to achieve world records through various creative and innovative methods.

A multifaceted person who can apply the best of his intellect using the God-given blessings which have been showered upon every human being granting them an immense capacity to learn, experience, and experiment with many things and do wonders in this world of discrimination and disparities.

He is a teacher and a student at the same time who always learns every day and teaches every day. As a master, his weakness was that he never sticks to a particular subject. Perhaps this weakness gives him the strength to master any area which he came across.

Each of his days dawned with learning a new topic and he spend most of his time experimenting and researching it.

He is also a selfless social activist and a motivational speaker.

His life was full of struggle, ups and downs, and failures.

But he never gave up and faced all his trials and tribulations full of confidence. Today he is a successful young man with a lot of enthusiasm and rich life experience.

He has sung full Ram Charita Manas 51 hours audio by his own composition. He has also sung the whole Bhagavad-Gita in his own composition with a rhythmic background.

He has also sung "Lokah Samastha Sukhino Bhavantu" in 50 different languages.

Currently working on a detailed and scientific study on Veda, Upanishad, Puranas, Bhagavad Gita, etc.

He has composed and sung Hanuman Chalisa in 108 different compositions and Gayatri Mantra in 1008 different compositions.

Awards

Four Times Guinness World Records

Winner of Mahatma Gandhi Vishwa Shanti Puraskar

Mahatma Gandhi Global Peace Ambassador

Kashi Ratna Award

Dr. APJ Abdul Kalam Motivational Person of the Year 2017

Mother Teresa Award

Indira Gandhi Priyadarshini Award

Bharat Vikas Ratna Award

Udyog Ratna Award

Vigyan Prasar Award

Poorvanchal Ratn Samman

Preface

No doubt, almost everyone in the world has heard of the Vedas, one of the most expansive literary treasuries of India. This book seeks to provide a concise and comprehensive understanding of the Vedas. It is an invaluable source of knowledge, offering insight into the ancient culture and traditions of India. It is a unique collection of wisdom, providing a glimpse into the spiritual and philosophical beliefs of the past. The Vedas are a timeless source of inspiration, offering guidance and enlightenment to those who seek it.

Here, I have attempted to provide a brief overview of the Vedas for basic understanding. The Vedas are a collection of ancient Indian texts, composed in Sanskrit, that are considered to be the oldest and most sacred scriptures of Hinduism. They are believed to have been composed by sages and seers over thousands of years, and are divided into four main categories: Rigveda, Yajurveda, Samaveda, and Atharvaveda. Each of these categories contains hymns, prayers, and rituals that are used in Hindu worship and religious ceremonies. The Vedas are also believed to contain spiritual and philosophical teachings that are still relevant today

Here, I have attempted to provide a brief overview of the Vedas for basic understanding.

Preface

No doubt, almost everyone in the world has heard of the Vedas, one of the most expansive literary treasures of India. This book seeks to provide a concise and comprehensive understanding of the Vedas. It is an invaluable source of knowledge, offering insight into the ancient culture and traditions of India. It is a unique collection of wisdom, providing a glimpse into the spiritual and philosophical beliefs of the past. The Vedas are a timeless source of [illegible], offering [illegible] and enlightenment [illegible] it.

Here, I have attempted to provide a brief overview of the Vedas for better understanding. The Vedas are a collection of ancient Indian texts, composed in Sanskrit. They are considered to be the oldest and most sacred scriptures of Hinduism. They are believed to have been composed [illegible] thousands of years ago and are divided into four parts, namely the Rigveda, Yajurveda, Samaveda, and Atharvaveda. [illegible] hymns, mantras and rituals that are used in Hindu worship and [illegible]. The Vedas are also believed to contain spiritual and philosophical teachings that are still relevant today.

Here, I have attempted to provide a brief overview of the Vedas for better understanding.

CHAPTER ONE

VEDAS - INTRODUCTION

The Vedas are a collection of ancient Sanskrit hymns, composed in India around 1500--1200 BCE. These hymns provide insight into the religious practices of the Vedic Period, and serve as one of the earliest known sources of Hinduism.

The Vedas are divided into four distinct collections; the Rigveda, Yajurveda, Samaveda, and Atharvaveda. The Rigveda is the oldest, and is composed of 1028 hymns dedicated to various Aryan gods and goddesses, such as Indra and Agni. It also contains prayers, magical spells, and divination spells. The Yajurveda is composed of sacrificial rituals and mantras. Its purpose was to aide in the performance of Vedic sacrifices. The Samaveda is a collection of tunes and melodies to be used during the presentation of these hymns. The Atharvaveda is the youngest of all the Vedas, and mostly consists of occult charms and spells for protection and healing.

The Vedas are also seen as integral parts of Hindu philosophy. They are seen as the beginning of philosophical enquiry, and offer teachings on a range of topics such as the nature of the universe, the soul, the Dharma (duty), and the relationship between the individual and the divine.

The Vedas have served as a priceless resource of knowledge and inspiration for generations of Hindus. These texts are seen as the foundations upon which Hinduism is built, and offer timeless wisdom that still resonates today. The Vedas are also referred to as the 'Veda Vyasa', or 'knowledge of the ages', due to their age and scope.

Most of the hymns in the Vedas are composed in a spiritual language and can only be understood by those initiated in the Vedic tradition; however, passages from them are frequently quoted in modern Hindu writing and sermons. They are held in high regard and are seen as a source of divine power and a way to connect with the divine.

The Vedas offer a unique insight into the worldview and culture of an ancient civilization, as well as providing timeless spiritual guidance. They are of immense importance in Hinduism, and are seen as the bedrock of all Hindu thought and practice.

CHAPTER TWO

HOW MANY VEDAS ARE THERE

There are four Vedas in the ancient Hindu religious texts, and they are often referred to as the four Vedic collections. The Vedas contain an immense amount of wisdom and guidance, and have been the foundation for countless traditions, cultures, and religions since ancient times. For Hindus, the Vedas are the most important scriptures, for they are the source of all truths and provide the paths for life.

The Rigveda is the oldest Veda, and it is the earliest collection of Vedic hymns and prayers that is still in use today. It is believed to have been composed between 1500 and 1200 BCE, and it contains more than a thousand hymns and 10,000 verses. The Rigveda is a collection of praises dedicated to the Vedic gods and goddesses, as well as offering deep philosophical thoughts and spiritual guidance on many topics.

The Sama Veda is a collection of Vedic mantras and hymns. It is believed to have been composed between 1400 and 1000 BCE, and is the second oldest Veda. It is shorter than the Rigveda and consists of 1,875 verses. The Sama Veda is primarily used for liturgical and ritualistic rituals and ceremonies.

The Yajurveda is the third Veda, and it is believed to have been composed between 1200 and 800 BCE. It is composed of 1,975 verses and is divided into two parts, the White Yajurveda and the Black Yajurveda. The White Yajurveda contains Mantra-related verses that were used during complex rituals and ceremonies, while the Black Yajurveda contains comprehensive prose formulas.

The Atharvaveda is the fourth and youngest Veda, and it is believed to have been composed between 800 and 600 BCE. It is composed of 1,176 verses and is believed to be the source of much of the ancient religion's ritualistic systems. It contains hymns and prayers associated with various aspects of life and the spiritual aspects of being.

The four Vedas are part of the Hindu Dharma, or religion, and have been part of the spiritual experience for centuries. They offer guidance, spiritual advice and help believers gain an understanding of the universe and the divine power that exists within it. They are considered to be the foundation for all Hinduism, and have been an integral part of the religion since ancient times. The Vedas continue to be studied and practiced by followers, and are an important part of the Hindu tradition and culture.

CHAPTER THREE

IMPORTANCE OF VEDAS

The Vedas are the oldest and most sacred texts of Hinduism and are some of the most influential ancient texts in the world. They are said to have been revealed by divine sources and are composed of four major texts. They are Rig-Veda, Yajur Veda, Sama Veda and Atharva Veda. The Vedas are revered by Hindus and are considered the foundational scriptures of Hinduism. They are also considered to be sacred to followers of Buddhism, Jainism, and Sikhism.

The Vedas are important for a variety of reasons. They provide an insight into the ancient Hindu culture and beliefs. They offer a vast array of spiritual knowledge that has been passed through the ages, from generation to generation. They provide the foundation for fundamental Hindu teachings, such as the four goals of life and the sacred practice of yoga. Furthermore, the Vedas are invaluable in providing an understanding of how Hindu philosophy and values have evolved over time.

The Vedas also provide an important source of moral

guidance for Hindus. They teach that dharma, or right action, must always be observed. This includes living a life of honesty and integrity, as well as striving to make ethical choices in all aspects of life. Additionally, the Vedas provide insight into the inherent spiritual nature of all things. This includes respect for the environment and all living beings, as well as the importance of leading a spiritual life.

The Vedas also offer an invaluable source of knowledge and wisdom. They contain a vast array of metaphysical knowledge and truths that can help guide individuals in their spiritual journeys. Additionally, they can provide insight into the metaphysical realms and dimensions, as well as the relationship between humans and the divine. The Vedas are also full of valuable advice and teachings that can be applied to life, such as meditation and yoga.

The Vedas are an important source of spiritual and moral knowledge that have been passed down for generations. They provide insight into ancient Hindu values and teachings and offer moral guidance for Hindus. Additionally, the Vedas contain a vast array of metaphysical and spiritual wisdom that can be applied to life. As such, the Vedas are highly revered by Hindus and considered to be of immense importance.

CHAPTER FOUR

VERSES IN VEDAS

The Vedas are a collection of ancient sacred texts and hymns that are believed to have been composed and collected in the Indian subcontinent between 1500 and 1000 BCE. These texts form an important part of the Hindu religious tradition, and largely encompass the philosophical and spiritual foundations of Hinduism.

The Vedas are composed mainly of verses, known as mantras, which have been revered, studied, and shared across generations. These verses are seen as a source of knowledge and wisdom, which have been passed down orally since ancient times and contain insights into human morality and the concept of a higher power.

The Vedas are divided into four distinct collections, or Samhitas, which are Rigveda, Samaveda, Yajurveda, and Atharvaveda. The Rigveda is the most ancient and revered of the four, having been composed around the 17th century BCE. It is composed of 1028 hymns in praise of various Hindu deities, particularly Indra, Agni and Soma. These hymns often contain a series of complex imagery, trying to capture the elusive concept of divine intervention in our lives.

The Samaveda is the second of the four Samhitas, and is an anthology of songs and chants that were used during Vedic rituals and ceremonies. These verses, known as gāyatrīmantras, are composed of Vedic phrases, mantras, and hymns. Unlike the Rigveda, the Samaveda is not as revered and often serves as an accompaniment to the Rigveda during rituals.

The Yajurveda is the third Veda and the longest of the four Samhitas. This collection of texts encompasses various rituals, hymns, and formulas that are used by priests in the Hindu religion. It is composed of recited words, used as a form of liturgy, rather than hymns and mantras as seen in the other collections.

The fourth and last collection is known as the Atharvaveda, and it is the shortest of the four Samhitas. It is composed of 731 hymns, prayers and spells, mostly focusing on charms and spells that offer protection from various ailments and problems. This collection is ancient and revered, and many of the mantras and verses contained within it are heavily used in Hindu religious ceremonies.

The Vedic verses contained within these four collections have been used throughout Hinduism for centuries, and are often used as a source of insight and inspiration for Hindus around the world. These mantras and hymns encapsulate many of the core beliefs, philosophies, and spiritual insights found within Hinduism, and provide a glimpse into the life and experiences of Hindus in ancient times.

CHAPTER FIVE

CONTENT OF VEDAS

The Vedas are the ancient Hindu scriptures, believed to be divine revelations, which have been thought to have been composed in the Indian subcontinent from 1500 BCE to 1200 BCE. The term 'Vedas' literally means knowledge or wisdom. The Vedas are composed in Sanskrit and can be divided into four primary collections known as the Rig, Yajur, Sama and Atharva. Each of these collections consists of a vast array of books written by different authors over an extended period of time.

The Rig Veda is the oldest and most important of the Vedas, believed to be composed between 1500 - 1000 BCE. The Rig Veda contains 1,017 hymns, many of which are dedicated to the worship of various gods and goddesses such as Agni, Indra, and Usha. The Rig Veda is a vital source of information about the ancient Indian culture and is the basis for many of the rituals and customs that form Hinduism today.

The Yajur Veda is believed to have been composed between 1000 - 800 BCE. The Yajur Veda consists of liturgy containing sacrificial prayers, mantras and formulas used for ceremonial purposes. It contains detailed instructions for animal and human sacrifices, as well as instructions for host rituals such as weddings and funerals. It is an important source of knowledge about ancient Indian rituals, ceremonies and beliefs about cosmic forces.

The Sama Veda is believed to have been composed between 800 - 500 BCE. The Sama Veda is composed primarily of songs and verses which were used in sacrificial ceremonies. The Sama Veda contains chants and mantras which were used in the worship of various gods, such as Agni and Indra, as well as of abstract cosmic forces. It is an important source of information on the spiritual practices of the Vedic period.

The Atharva Veda is believed to have been composed between 500 - 400 BCE. The Atharva Veda consists mainly of magical formulas, charms and incantations used for various purposes. It is an important source of information about the belief in ghosts and other supernatural forces, as well as their use in religious ceremonies.

The Vedas also contain philosophical texts and narratives which are believed to have been added to the Vedas after their initial compilation. These texts offer insights into the beliefs and thoughts of the ancient Hindus, as well as a valuable source of information on their views on the nature of the self, God and the universe.

The Vedas provide invaluable insight into the beliefs and practices of the ancient peoples of the Indian subcontinent. They are a source of great religious, philosophical and cultural significance, and remain invaluable to Hindu traditions even today.

CHAPTER SIX

WHAT WE CAN LEARN FROM VEDAS

The Vedas are a collection of prayers and hymns from ancient India composed between around 1300 and 1100 BCE, from authors whose names are now unknown. They are the key scriptures of Hinduism and an important source of Indian culture and tradition. The Vedas provide an intricate account of the religious and spiritual teachings of the ancient sages of India.

One of the primary teachings of the Vedas is the notion of Dharma. Dharma is the spiritual law that governs all things, linking mankind to their divine order. Essentially, it is a code of right conduct meant to guide humanity on its path to the divine. Dharma is the foundation of what it means to lead a life that is aligned with the divine. According to the Vedas, true Dharma arises from an understanding of the ultimate truth that God exists in all aspects of life.

The Vedas also state that the goal of life is to strive for spiritual perfection. The Vedic sages taught that the purpose of life is to cultivate a deep connection to the sacred through living with awareness and compassion. As part of this process, the Vedic sages emphasized the importance of sacred rituals and practices. They taught that performing rituals and offering sacrifices to the Gods was a way to nourish and maintain this bond.

In addition to Dharma and spiritual perfection, the Vedas also provide guidance on the pursuit of other positive qualities such as humility, respect, and compassion. It is believed that by developing these qualities, one is able to become a harmonious part of the cosmic order. As part of this teaching, the Vedas also emphasize the importance of maintaining harmonious relations with others.

The Vedas also propose many ethical practices for leading a good life. This includes the observance of codes such as Ahimsa (non-violence) and Satyam (truthfulness). This is a reminder that even simple actions can reflect your connection to the divine. The Vedic sages believed that by following these codes, one would create a life filled with joy, peace and love.

Finally, the Vedic sages taught the concept of Moksha or liberation from the cycle of birth and death. In the Vedic teachings, Moksha is the highest spiritual goal and is attained through spiritual transformation. The Vedas emphasizes that the ideal state of Moksha is achieved by enlightenment, or by realizing the ultimate truth: we are all connected as part of a cosmic order.

In summary, the Vedas are a collection of ancient religious and spiritual teachings of the Vedic sages of India, and provide powerful lessons on living a life of Dharma, spiritual perfection and ethical practices. By understanding these teachings, we can lead a life in harmony with the divine and create a more peaceful, joyful and enlightened world.

CHAPTER SEVEN

SIGNIFICANCE OF VEDAS

The Vedas are a collection of sacred texts written in Sanskrit, with origins believed to date back more than 4,000 years. They are the revered scriptures of the Hindu religion, which encompasses the beliefs and practices of more than one billion people worldwide. The Vedas are believed to contain universal knowledge, transmitted by a lineage of sages and kept in oral form for thousands of years. In modern times, the Vedas are published and available in written form. As such, they provide an essential source of guidance to those who wish to explore and develop a deeper understanding of the foundations of Hindu faith and spirituality.

The Vedas are divided into four large collections, or Samhitas. The first of these is the Rigveda, which is the oldest of the Vedas. It includes compositions of hymns, prayers, and religious formulae, and is a major source of knowledge regarding the Vedic deities and rituals. The second Samhita is the Yajurveda, which is a collection of sacrificial formulas and liturgical instructions on rites and ceremonies. It is closely related to the Rigveda, and provides further detail on the practices prescribed therein. The third Samhita is the Samaveda, which is a musical collection of hymns from the Rigveda arranged in such a way as to be sung for special occasions and rituals. The fourth and final Samhita is the Atharvaveda, which provides further information on the spiritual and magical aspects of Hindu rituals, including charms and incantations.

Of all the Samhitas, the Rigveda is considered to be the most important and is often referred to as the "Veda of Knowledge". It is believed to embody the essence of the entire Vedic tradition and is said to contain the sum total of all Vedic knowledge. At the same time, it is important to note that each of the Samhitas is incredibly valuable in its own right, and collectively they provide a comprehensive overview of the Vedic way of life.

The Vedas also contain a range of sub-texts which help to explain and showcase the complexity and breadth of Vedic knowledge. These include Upanishads, Aranyakas, Brahmanas, Smritis and various Sutras. The Upanishads are philosophical texts that explore the deeper meaning of life, and the Aranyakas provide a transition between Vedic rituals and the mysticism of the Upanishads. The Brahmanas prescribe methods for performing rituals, the Smritis are codes of social, moral and legal conduct, and various Sutra texts include aphorisms on specific topics.

The Vedas are an invaluable source of information and represent a vast body of knowledge. They have greatly shaped culture, religion and spirituality in India, and continue to inform and guide those who take the time to explore their teachings.

CHAPTER EIGHT

VEDAS CONNECTION WITH UPANISHAD

The Vedas and Upanishads are considered foundational texts in Indian philosophy, and are widely regarded as some of the oldest literature on earth. They are both revered for their spiritual and religious teachings, but many people don't understand the connection between the two texts. In order to understand how these two works of ancient wisdom are related, it is first important to define their purposes.

The Vedas are a collection of hymns and mantras performed and written by ancient practitioners of Hinduism around 1,500-2,000 B.C. While these Vedic texts were mainly created for the purpose of worship and spiritual practices, they also contain some of the earliest literature on philosophy and religion written in the Sanskrit language. The four Vedas, Rig-Veda, Yajur-Veda, Sama-Veda, and Atharva-Veda, each speaks to different topics related to philosophy, religion, cosmology, nature, and more.

The Upanishads, written between 1000 and 500 B.C., are

a collection of ancient philosophical treatises that pursue philosophical questions on the nature of life, existence, and the nature of the soul. The Upanishads are composed of discussions between teachers and students, and many of the questions explored are similar to those found in western philosophy.

So how are the Vedas and Upanishads connected? According to scholars, the Upanishadic writers used the teachings from the Vedas as the starting point for many of their discussions and drew upon the Vedic materials in order to explore new philosophical questions. In other words, the Upanishads were built upon the Vedas. The Vedic hymns and mantras created a shared worldview and set of spiritual experiences that were the foundation for the philosophical investigations found in the Upanishads. The authors of the Upanishads link the concepts of the Vedas to the core Upanishadic concept of moksha (liberation or self-realization).

The Vedas and Upanishads can therefore be seen as both distinct and complimentary texts. While distinct in content, they both support each other in teaching ancient Hindu beliefs and enlightening us on the nature of life and existence. The Vedas provide a spiritual foundation from which the Upanishads go on to explore more philosophical questions. Together, these two texts create an understanding of one of mankind's oldest cultures and its relationship to the spiritual world.

CHAPTER NINE

VEDA'S CONNECTION WITH BHAGAVADGITA

The Vedas and the Bhagavad Gita are two of the most important scriptures of Hinduism, and they have a deep connection. The Vedas have been considered the foundation of Hinduism, and they are an ancient collection of religious and spiritual texts. The Bhagavad Gita, on the other hand, is a portion of the epic poem the Mahabharata, and it contains the teachings of Krishna to Arjuna. Both texts offer valuable insight into the foundation and nature of Hinduism.

The Vedas are a collection of four texts, the Rig Veda, Yajur Veda, Sama Veda and Atharva Veda. They focus on prayers and rituals that were used for worship and essential instructions on the right way of living. The Vedas contain the basis of Hindu philosophy, a set of eternal truths and values. They are believed to have been passed down by word-of-mouth, and they are still used today in rituals and ceremonies.

The Bhagavad Gita is a part of the Mahabharata, and it is one of the most well known pieces of Hindu scripture. The Bhagavad Gita is the conversation between the god Krishna and the warrior Arjuna. Krishna gives Arjuna advice on how to effectively combat his enemies, but the underlying message is about life and how to live according to the teachings of Vedas. The advice Krishna gives centers around the idea of karma, or actions, and how important it is to live according to the teachings of Vedas.

The Vedas and Bhagavad Gita are intimately connected as the latter is a comment on the teaching of the former. It explains these Vedic teachings in a modern way, elaborating on the importance of living according to these eternal truths. The Bhagavad Gita is an expansion of these Vedic teachings and is still very relevant today. It is read and studied by many, providing spiritual guidance on how to live a good life.

The Vedas and the Bhagavad Gita both provide essential guidance on living a good life and following Hindu spirituality. The Vedas give eternal truths and values that have been passed down over time, while the Bhagavad Gita is a commentary of these teachings, elaborating on the importance of living according to them. Together, the Vedas and the Bhagavad Gita provide Hindus with valuable guidance for all aspects of life.

CHAPTER TEN

CONNECTION OF VEDAS WITH PURANAS

The ancient scriptures of India, known collectively as the Vedas, are the oldest texts to be recordcd in thc Indian subcontinent. The Vedas, a compilation of ancient hymns, prayers, and chants, are a vast body of wisdom that establishes the foundations for much of the subsequent Indian traditions and beliefs. While the Vedas are sources of great spiritual knowledge, they also connect, in important ways, to the Puranas, a body of Hindu literature that expounds upon the history of the universe and the adventures of divine gods, goddesses, and creatures.

The connection between the Vedas and the Puranas is found in their shared references to the same deities and belief systems. The Vedas, for example, mention many of the same aspects of Hinduism that are featured in the Puranas, such as the gods and goddesses of the Hindu pantheon, the power of the holy trinity, and the concept of karma and reincarnation. Similarly, the Puranas elaborate upon the tales and stories mentioned in the Vedas, providing descriptions of the gods and goddesses, their relationships to one another, and their adventures. This profound connection between the Vedas and the Puranas illustrates the longevity of the Hindu faith and the consistent cultural beliefs that pervade the Indian subcontinent.

This connection is further demonstrated in the structure of the Puranas themselves, which are divided into two main categories: the “sargas” and the “upavedas”. Sargas, which are narratives told through the eyes of human characters, usually detail the adventures of the gods and goddesses, while upavedas, which are more formative accounts that explain the official doctrines of the Hindu faith, refer often to the Vedas. In other words, the upavedas use the ancient wisdom of the Vedas to describe the way in which Hinduism should be practiced by its followers.

In this way, the connection between the Vedas and the Puranas is clear and serves an important purpose in India. By linking the oldest and most fundamental religious texts with the modern beliefs of present-day Hindus, the connection helps to ensure the continuity and purity of the faith as it has been handed down through generations. In this way, the Vedas and the Puranas provide a valuable resource for Hindus looking to honor and understand the sacred origins of their faith.

CHAPTER ELEVEN

VEDA AND YOGA

The ancient Indian religious texts, The Vedas, are a collection of texts believed to be the oldest scriptures and scriptures in the world. Written between 1500 and 1000 B.C. in Sanskrit and concerned with the origins of Hinduism, the Vedas have had a significant impact on spiritual, educational and social customs in India, and around the world. Yoga, a system of practice that combines physical exercises, breathing techniques, and meditative techniques, is an integral part of the Indian spiritual tradition. While there is much debate and speculation about the precise relationship between the Vedas and Yoga, there are strong parallels between the two systems of thought.

The Vedas contain some of the earliest known descriptions of yogic postures and poses, attesting to the significant place of yoga in ancient India. In particular, the Vedas describe mudras, physical postures and hand gestures used to induce awareness and spiritual transformation. The Sanskrit word, yoga, means "to yoke," suggesting that the practices were designed to bring a person into harmony of body and mind. This aligns perfectly with the teachings of the Vedas, whose principal aim was to promote inner enlightenment, freedom and physical well-being.

Modern yogic practice draws very heavily on the Vedas, with many of the yoga poses originating in ancient India's spiritual tradition. This includes a wide variety of postures, designs and breathing exercises. Most classical yoga schools also teach meditation, another practice that finds its roots in the Vedas. The ancient scriptures contain descriptions of the meditative state and its benefits in cultivating awareness and clarity of thought.

The physical and spiritual elements of yogic practice are both rooted in the Vedic tradition. All forms of yoga share the same intention – to strengthen the connection between the individual and the divine, or ultimate reality. As such, the goal of yoga today is still very much in line with the message of the Vedas, which has survived for thousands of years.

Yoga, without a doubt, is deeply rooted in the Vedic tradition, but yogis today have taken this ancient practice in many new directions, incorporating elements from other spiritual practices and adapting it to the needs of their own students and societies. One could argue that this reflects the universal nature of yoga: that it is designed to be able to adapt to different contexts and cultures, but always maintain its core message. Undoubtedly, this core message is thanks, in part, to the teachings of the Vedas.

CHAPTER TWELVE

VEDIC RISHIES

Throughout history, Vedic rishis have been the guiding lights of ancient Indian culture. As the protectors of sacred knowledge, they have bequeathed generations with invaluable insights on philosophy, spirituality, governance, and science. They have played a great role in shaping the spiritual and ethical values of the Indian subcontinent and serve as revered figures in Hindus, Buddhists, and Jains alike. They also form the cornerstone of many ancient texts including the Vedas and Upanishads, providing an invaluable source of wisdom for seekers of Vedic knowledge.

The Vedic rishis were the first group of learned spiritual teachers and sages in India. It was believed that they were of lofty spiritual stature, having access to insight and understanding beyond the reach of ordinary people. They were historically revered for their expertise in both spiritual and temporal matters; they were considered to have had a direct connection to supernatural worlds, such as the celestial realms.

The Vedic rishis were instrumental in preserving sacred spiritual knowledge and passing it down through generations. This allowed the Hindu faith to remain strong and vibrant, despite centuries of cultural and foreign influence. Furthermore, their influence on matters like morality and philosophy was greatly appreciated by the people.

The teachings of the Vedic rishis are very relevant in today's world. Besides providing immense knowledge in the realm of scripture and spiritual practice, they have prescribed principles that can be practical and beneficial. The core teachings of Vedic rishis involve how to live in harmony with nature, how to protect the environment, how to sustain ethical behaviour, how to attain spiritual development, and how to find inner peace.

Additionally, the Vedic rishis have contributed greatly to the holistic well-being of humankind. Most of their ancient teachings were based on physical, mental, and fifth dimensional well-being, aiming towards achieving balance in the three bodies and finding joy both inside and outside. By instilling a sense of responsibility for their own thoughts, words and actions, the Vedic rishis taught that individuals could positively affect their environment by being mindful of the consequences of their thoughts, words and actions.

It is undeniable that the teachings and insights of the Vedic rishis are still relevant today and serve as a rich source of inspiration and guidance. Their timeless and invaluable wisdom continues to shed light and guide humanity on the path of truth and growth. Through their guidance and teachings, the Vedic rishis have served as a powerful reminder of the importance of self-realization and the power of positivity in all aspects of our lives, including our physical, mental, emotional and spiritual health.

CHAPTER THIRTEEN

VEDAS IN A NUTSHELL AS A SUMMARY

The Vedas are the most ancient religious texts of Hinduism and play a foundational role in the religion. These scriptures originated in India at least 3,000 years ago and form the basis of Hindu religious doctrines, rituals, and practices. Modern Hinduism is largely based on the four Vedas: the Rigveda, Yajurveda, Samaveda, and Atharvaveda.

The Rigveda is the oldest of the four Vedas and is considered the most sacred of the texts. It is composed of hymns, mantras, and prayers, and is seen as a collection of divine revelations covering a variety of topics, including mythology and cosmology, what it means to be human, cosmic order and laws, and a call to follow the divine path of dharma.

The Yajurveda is composed of rituals and sacrificial formulas and was used to aid in religious ceremonies. It is an extensive record of rituals related to the sacrifice of offerings to gods, their associated chants and formulas, and instructions for performing the sacrifices.

The Samaveda is the third Veda and is composed of musical chants set to various meters and notes. This literature is used to accompany sacrificial rituals, as well as for personal reflection and meditation.

The Atharvaveda is the fourth and last Veda and is composed of hymns, spells, and charms. It is considered the darkest of the Vedic scriptures as it deals with mysticism, black magic, and the practice of exorcism.

In the Vedic tradition, the Vedas are seen as an unchanging source of spiritual knowledge and the ultimate authority in matters of religious debate and investigation. It is believed that these texts contain timeless wisdom and the ultimate truth about the universe, one that is revealed through their careful study and scrutiny.

The Vedas also influence many aspects of Hindu culture and traditions, including many of its major festivals, social customs, and ceremonies. The Vedas are revered in the Hindu faith and it is believed that a person's spiritual journey begins with the Rigveda, progresses through Yajurveda and ends with Atharvaveda.

In summary, the Vedas are ancient scriptures which form the basis of the Hindu religion. They contain timeless wisdom and truths about the universe and influence many aspects of Hindu culture and traditions. The Vedas are seen as an unchanging source of spiritual knowledge and are revered in the Hindu faith.

CHAPTER FOURTEEN

VEDAS CONNECTION WITH AYURVEDA

Ayurveda is a holistic system of natural medicine derived from ancient Indian scriptures, known as the Vedas. This traditional form of healing is based on the concept of balancing the energies in the body, mind, and spirit to create a state of health and well-bcing. Thc Vedas are the oldest known collection of sacred texts in Hinduism and are believed to contain divine knowledge and understanding of the physical, mental, and spiritual world.

The Vedas contain several references to the use of herbal remedies for the promotion of health and healing. These ancient scriptures also provide descriptions of the optimal methods of self-care and prevention of disease. This system of healing was developed from a combination of the different disciplines described in the Vedas, including yogic practice, herbal medicines, and prayer.

The Vedas provide extensive guidance for practitioners of Ayurveda in diagnosing, assessing, and treating various types of illnesses. The texts provide Ayurvedic practitioners with detailed information regarding the health of patients and specific instructions on how to use various herbal remedies in various treatments.

The Vedas also list various foods that were traditionally used to maintain health and prevent diseases. Many of these items are still used today in Ayurvedic treatments and are believed to have healing properties.

The Vedic scriptures also provide Ayurvedic practitioners with detailed descriptions of the physical and spiritual effects of various types of treatments. These descriptions provide insight into the connection between the body and the mind, allowing practitioners to develop a personalized approach to treatment. This connection ensures that treatments are tailored to the individual needs of each patient.

The Vedas also provide beneficial guidance and advice to those who wish to practice Ayurveda. This includes advice on how to lead a holistic and healthy life, with emphasis on harmonizing the physical, mental, and spiritual aspects of life.

In conclusion, the Vedas have served as the foundation for Ayurveda for thousands of years, providing a detailed understanding of health and well-being and providing practitioners with information and advice to help their patients achieve and maintain health. The Vedas offer invaluable knowledge for understanding the connection between the body and the mind and for treating various physical and spiritual conditions. This understanding is key to successfully utilizing the practice of Ayurveda.

Contact

9839093003

myrichindia@gmail.com

drjagadeeshpillai@facebook

jagadeeshpillai@youtube

www.JAGADEESHPILLAI.com

Printed by Libri Plureos GmbH in Hamburg, Germany